Out of the Ashes

Also by Jill Gloyne and published by Ginninderra Press
Brushstrokes

Jill Gloyne
Out of the Ashes

Out of the Ashes
ISBN 978 1 76041 684 3
Copyright © text Jill Gloyne 2019
Cover photo: Miriam Espacio via StockSnap

First published 2019 by
GINNINDERRA PRESS
PO Box 3461 Port Adelaide 5015 Australia
www.ginninderrapress.com.au

This book is dedicated to Bernie Mazrat

Out of the Ashes

The bush doesn't know what awaits it,
lying in the bowl of this heated cauldron.
Giant gums, arms outstretched,
plead for the cool of the evening,
shedding their bark like discarded corsets;
bush pods pop like Indian spice
in a hot dry wok;
kangaroos doze in the shade;
insects, in a maze of frenzy
rush to escape the echidna's tongue;
a magpie pecks at a pile of leaves
as thick and dry as long-lost memory;
wrens twitter and flit, uneasy
in this beleaguered air.

On the far horizon
a setting sun stretches out like flames
along the windowsill of the indigo night
waiting for tomorrow to open.

Theoretically,
council regulations
will not let you
gather your firewood
from the roadside.

Theoretically,
if you leave it there,
long enough,
the inferno will be spectacular;
it will burn hotter,
spread faster,
and turn more living things
into unrecognisable
charcoal.

National parks like to keep fires to themselves.
They don't believe in cool burning for weeds,
don't like disturbing the vegetation with firebreaks.
And they don't like Elvis dumping salt water on their ground.

But the trouble is –
when fire finally breaks out,
after fuming and festering for days,
all Hell's let loose on land
that should have been saved.

It should have been a normal working day,
a day like any other. And so it was at first.
But then, that sudden flash of lightning,
the fiery bolt that unzips flames from hell,
torches crops, turns dreams to dust,
swallows the air we need to breathe,
and smudges out all future hopes
with an ear-splitting roar…

Oh! the deafening sound
of that tunnel of fire
as it covers the ground
until all in its pathway is
blackened or browned.

It should have been a day like any other,
forgotten in the mundane course of life.
But no.
Seared onto the lens of memory
it can never be peeled off,
discarded,
or forgotten.

The day dawns bright and burning hot:
is that the siren I hear?
The heat is so bad it could char your soul
with the silent pulse of fear.

The heat is so bad it could char your soul.
Is that the siren I hear?
In the dead, dry bush the animals hide
in silent dread and fear.

In the dead, dry bush the animals hide.
Is that the siren I hear?
Aware that their world is about to change
 with its silent pulse of fear.

Aware that their world is about to change.
Is that the siren I hear?
Men swarm around the CFS
in silent dread and fear.

Men swarm around the CFS.
Is that the siren I hear?
Like ants abandoning their nests
in the silent pulse of fear.

Like ants abandoning their nests.
Is that the siren I hear?
They leave to fight that fickle fire
in silent dread and fear.

They leave to fight that fickle fire.
Is that the siren I hear?
They know not where the flames will lead
with their silent pulse of fear.

They know not where the flames will lead.
Is that the siren I hear?
But they'll fight to save their stock and land
in silent dread and fear.

They'll fight to save their stock and land.
Is that the siren I hear?
They'll fight throughout the day, the night
with the silent pulse of fear.

They'll fight throughout the day and night.
Is that the siren I hear?
Not knowing what they'll find next day
what silence, dread and fear.

Not knowing what they'll find next day.
Is that the siren I hear?
What will be lost, what will be saved
in the silent pulse of fear.

What will be lost, what will be saved,
is that the siren I hear?
Will their world be draped in an ash-grey hush
with silent dread and fear?

Will their world be draped in an ash-grey hush?
Is that the siren I hear,
telling the toll of the land that they love
and its silent pulse of fear?

Jim Mcfarlane awoke
to the sound of the siren
and said to his wife,
'It's wailing like a bloody banshee.'

He drove to the local CFS,
struggling with his clothes as he went,
thinking it was just another fire,
that he'd be home for tea.

Jim McFarlane had never thought
about fire and transformation.
If anyone had said to him:
'Fire can turn dross to gold, you know,

like Phoenix rising from the ashes,'
he would have replied –
or perhaps just thought –
'You're bloody barmy, mate.'

But on the day Jim McFarlane
answered the banshee's call,
his life was about to change forever.

Like bees returning to their queen
men buzz around in a hive of activity.
Every act, every movement,
instinctive, automatic, practised,
years of training in motion;
phones ring with the latest reports,
orders are given or altered accordingly
and positions are manned for the fray,
all in response to the day's category:

Catastrophic.

Then the wailing firetrucks leave
to fight an unfettered inferno;
while the faces of women preparing the food
wear the wooden fear of widowhood.

Like an old crone's cackle the ancient gums crackle,
sparks and flames leap, surreptitiously creep
in whispering grass and with a sigh pass
like a wild orange ball in a thickening pall
of heavy grey smoke that suffocates, chokes,
blinds weary eyes, mantles all cries,
while the heat all around with an ear-splitting sound
like the flapping of sails coming loose in a gale,
whiplashes ears, fills hearts with fear,
for the fiery winds know they can choose where they go
while man can but aim at those fingers of flame
with hoses adancing to stem their advancing.
And when it is over an ashen white cover
spreads over a landscape devoid of all hope
while a silence that hums on throbbing eardrums
like the solitary call of a black crow is all
that is left of the world where this fury unfurled.

The fire that day would etch
staccato memories into forgetfulness,
like an echo calling back,
involuntarily, over the passing years.
Fickle winds fired up the flames
in a St Vitus dance from east to west
then back again and off to somewhere else.

Day and night, night and day
they laboured with a hopeless hope
wrung out of living strength.

When Jim leapt out to open a gate
he tripped and fell,
collapsing into a world
he would willingly have left,
and nearly did,
as the merciless fire
engulfed them all.

Get the Flying Doctor, mate,
he's in an awful bloody state.
You'd better go to Adelaide, Lou,
be there for him when he comes to.

And so she left, bewildered by
the fact that Jim might even die,
and though they tried to give her hope
she didn't know how she would cope.

She'd seen him briefly passing by
all bandaged up and wondered why
of all the volunteers, just Jim
had suffered from the firestorm's whim.

It was a fear that gripped her tight,
she wanted him so much that night,
not as a fire-damaged escapee,
but the handsome man he used to be.

Unlike the outside world
everything's artificial
in the windowless ICU,
and the fight for life
is not a quiet one.
Lights flash and beep
their secret codes,
machines grow twisted tubes
like an octopus in *Dr Who*,
and they suck and sigh
with a regularity
that does not reflect the life
they're trying to save.
If only they could stop and cough,
just occasionally, mimic the life
they're frightened of losing,
anything to bring a sense of normality
back to this sterile world of control.

So, you've come back to us at last
I'm pleased to see. I'm Doctor Tim.
I'll be in charge of you when you leave here
for the ward where we treat burns.

You'll be there quite a while you know,
skin grafts can be tricky.
Your hands will heal, no problem there,
but your face…well, we'll just see.

The fire…? The fire…? It's out now, mate.
You've been unconscious several days.
The damage? Several homes and sheds
and stock of course, five thousand sheep I think.

And me? How long? How bad?
Ah, here's your wife. I'll leave you now…
Just try to rest. We'll do our best.
And please, don't worry.

The hand she holds is bandaged
so she cannot feel his skin
nor can she see his lovely face,
just three sad holes that might have been

gouged out from a ball of gauze.
If only, she thinks, they could touch
just like they used to do –
the touch that made her senses rush

as if in the passionate heat of love.
But everything is different here.
Their sad eyes wander, aimless, lost
on dead-end roads that don't know where

to meet. And their voices, so forlorn,
hang between them like a fireproof door,
a barrier they both must broach
to return to what they were before.

They feel so lost in this foreign land,
together it seems, yet far apart,
and the worst thing is they just don't know
how to find their way, how to make a start.

Christ, you wouldn't believe
what they do to you in here.
Bloody well staple the grafts on
like you were a piece of paper.
Every few weeks they take a sliver,
yes, just a sliver, they say, of your skin,
till you feel like a bloody raw onion.
Your body weeps and your eyes sting
as if you've just been shoved
through a plate glass door.
Then they bandage your face again,
all but your eyes and mouth
so they can feed you, keep you alive,
when all you really want
is just to fuckin' well die.

This'll make you laugh.
I now have ears on my eyes!
What, your eyes can hear?
I hear you ask. What a bonus.
Not really, mate.

My eyelids, badly burnt,
had to be remade so they could close
and the skin graft? You guessed it,
came from behind my ears,
where it was good as new.

It's funny you know, about grafts.
When I feel a scar which once
adorned my bum or thigh,
I think I can feel where it came from.
But I guess it's just imagination.

As for my ears, I know I'll never hear
what I want to hear again.
Nor will I see what I'd like to see,
let alone feel what I used to feel.

The nurses in the ward all knew
the height of the mountain he'd have to climb,
the length of the road he'd need to unwind
and then remake anew.

They were well aware it would take a while,
this was their job, they'd done it before.
Compassion would need to underscore
each act, each word, each smile.

Sometimes they hummed his favourite tunes,
removing his bandages with care,
gently treating his wounds before
rewinding the tape anew.

They hoped he would finally find the song
he needed to sing on his new-found road;
that different words and deeper tones
would one day make him strong.

The girl with her hair in a bun
reminds me of Miss Fischer in Grade 3,
but not quite so severe.
This one has little curls around her face,
ringlets of piglet tails
and she's not grey either.
When she smiles, her eyes light up
like Lou's used to.
I'm here from Social Welfare, she says,
Cenrelink, to see if I can help.
Help? By God, I wish you could,
but then, I guess you're a city girl
(her fingernails were painted green)
not versed in country ways.
You see, my dear,
I'm up to my neck in debt,
but my assets negate any assistance
that might be flying around
like the odd homing pigeon.
My mortgage gives me more despair
than you could ever imagine.
But thanks, anyway, for the visit,
I don't get many, you know.
Forms to fill out? Well, why not,
got nothing else to do.

Lou doesn't come to visit now.
She did at first. But then one day
they took my face mask off to show
her that my grafts were a success.

Successful's not the word I'd use.
What I saw behind her eyes
was worse than any ugly scar
I might have had.

She couldn't speak. She froze like ice,
recoiled in horror like she'd seen
a thing too horrible to touch,
a vision of a voiceless scream…

a scream that echoed silently,
dragging our love through cutting blades –
leaving it bleeding, God knows where,
but lifeless, heartless, soulless, dead.

Without a word, she turned and left,
leaving me alone, bereft.

Don't go, I wanted to call her back,
but she had fled, forever gone.

I pleaded with a nurse – Give me a mirror, girl,
I need to know what everyone's been hiding.

Reluctantly she handed me her makeup mirror.
Fuckin' Hell, a monster stared right back at me.
My eyes aren't even level. My right one,
dragging down, pulls against all future hope
that one day I might be a normal man again.
A dozer's gouged a path across my scalp,
too wide for the bush on either side
to meet again, to cover up my shame.
My face could be a patchwork quilt,
its stitches torn, awry, as if cobbled together
in a hurry by some careless hand
that's never heard of invisible mending.

Jim stared and stared at the ugly truth
the nurses knew they could no longer hide,
and then they saw him slowly clench his fist
and bring it down with all his force
upon that cursed mirror, leaving
a pile of worthless bloody shards.

Once a week the Big Chief comes.
Trussed like a chicken I await the chef.
My feet, flattened by envelope corners,
slowly begin to cramp,
pins and needles stitch a patch
of numbness to my bottom.
I dare not move, I might
rumple Sister's pride and joy;
a row of beds like coffins, so neat
you don't notice patients in them.
Which is why the white coats,
hovering like spectres at my feet,
speak over my head
to their wide-eyed students
as if I'm just a textbook.
And that's their world, all black and white.
They only see my burns, my scars,
not the underlying pain and loss
of my real world,
my deeply scarred and grey-toned world.

Who would have thought that biro lines
could cut him open like a sword,
that words could foster
grief and anger,
tear him apart
and toss him into
the eye of the storm.

In the silence of shock,
the sum of his sorrow wells
into sadness overflowing from his eyes,
like a dam after winter rain.

A nurse walks by,
comes to sit beside him.
She takes his hand.
Bad news? she asks.
He doesn't speak.
She strokes his arm
as if it's soft, warm velvet,
not rough, harsh canvas.
Eventually he replies:
My wife wants a divorce.
Some words cannot be answered.
She keeps on stroking his arm.

A female psychiatrist is on her way
to solve all my problems.
Can she bring Lou back to me?
Remove my scars?
Run the farm?
Might as well try
to pick up the night
when it falls at the end of day.
Fair crack of the whip –
I know I'm on my own,
I know I've got to be strong,
I know I've got to think positive,
balance on that tightrope
above the abyss of depression
until I get back to normalcy.
But for Christ's sake,
what's fuckin' normal, anyway?
Give me mates any day,
whether
normal or not.

J McFarlane. Report. 20.4.1983
Interview: Uncooperative.
Medication for pain demanded.
Medication for depression refused.
Cause of depression:
Fury (unresolved) at his situation,
Antagonism towards psychiatric help.
Requests no further consults.
Latent problems require resolution.
Anger appears based on wife's desertion.
Not amenable to any suggestions.
Exhibits signs of post-traumatic stress.

Lost in his world of sorrow and self-pity
he strayed with leaden steps into a mire.
His future was a subject he refused
to contemplate for it could never be
just like his past.
                            Were it not for his friends,
who knows what might have happened. But their visits
slowly cheered him; local gossip, wives'
and mothers' home-made cooking, smuggled beer
and cigarettes and plans for future jobs.

They travelled many miles to visit him
as if joined by a bond they could not break,
and when at last he talked of home, they knew
they'd brought him back from some dark foreign place
they didn't know themselves, but yet had feared.

When Jim was pronounced
fit to go home
joy spread throughout the ward.
Like a gradual transformation that
lightens the sadness in eyes and
rubs out furrows on a worried brow,
Jim's expression slowly changed.

His mates arrived with stubbies
and the nurses joined in too.
I'll bring your FJ over if you like.
I would, thanks Bill, I really would,
can't wait to get behind the wheel again.

But when he did he'd be setting out slowly
on a road that was both untravelled and lonely.

Let's call in to the pub for a beer.
But that wasn't really a good idea.
The young girls there, although they tried
to chat and to laugh, their words soon died.

It hit him hard that girls now thought
that he was changed. He knew they ought
to realise that 'neath his skin,
whether scarred or not, he was still just Jim.

So he left the pub and drove on home,
feeling utterly bitter and sad and alone.

The empty house was hard to face.
Lou's things had gone, and half the furniture.
It was no more a happy home,
a haven and a shelter from the storm.

Sad and solitary he stood,
his new world falling in on him,
like a flimsy house of cards –
and then he heard it:
the whine of a gear with a missing cog,
the scratch at the door of a faithful dog
who'd been next door for months.
'Twas Bob his border collie
helped Jim through that sorry night.
He licked his scars, then licked again,
his tongue a healing balm
to soothe the pain of what had been
far worse than all those fiery flames.

They sat together on the lounge,
and talked till all was said,
while the harvest moon, in the darkening sky
entwined their shadows and tossed them on high
to the other side of the stream nearby
where they drowned in the curlew's mournful cry.

Blinded by the burning blade of a
morning sun which he could not
feel on his scars, he thought –
if only the wounds in my heart
were as numb as my hideous face
perhaps I would not feel so fraught
with bitterness and fear.

He gathered up his documents,
the records that once gave him joy
and with leaden steps set slowly off
for a visit he'd rather avoid.
Got to see the bank now, Bob,
he said as he passed by.
And when he ruffled his best mate's coat
he thought he saw in the old dog's eye
the flickering hope of a lighthouse beam
reaching out to a stormy sea and sky.

He'd had six months to think, to plan,
but this wasn't a game of Monopoly.
The boss at the bank, with worthless words,
confirmed what he already knew,
but hoped, in vain, would not be true.

Divorces don't come cheap, you know.
To pay out what you must
you'll have to sell the farm.
You can't increase your mortgage
and survive. Survive? he thought.
Survive? I wish I bloody well hadn't.

You've been on borrowed time
for several years, he heard.
If only he could really borrow time,
he thought, a time that's interest free.
Let's hope you find a buyer soon.

And that was the sum of
the manager's consolation,
his voice as flat as someone
reading an instruction chart
to tired and bored apprentices.
And then, that final insult, a flabby palm,
to a man who's handshake,
his word, his bond,
could have, quite easily,
broken a metacarpal or two.

So he sold the farm at a bargain price
to pay out Lou her due,
found a job on a shearing team
with work the whole year through.

He bought a second-hand caravan,
a home for him and Bob.
A different life, a different world,
where he'd move around with his job.

He'd given his future considerable thought;
this life on a different scale,
now all that was left was to pack things up
and then, the clearing sale.

For better or worse, he knew he had no choice
but sort and pack, discard his former life.
It's like a death, he thought, as he went through
his former years, each object with its halo
of suspended memory. The clock he loved,
his grandad's wedding present, now run down,
as if awaiting Jim to turn the key,
restart it once again. And other things
he needed to hold on to for a while
as if to let them go too soon would be
like swallowing food that goes the wrong
way down, and sticks.
                       It took him several days
to sort out what to keep, to sell, to burn,
a job he never thought could be so hard.
And when the task was done, he packed his clothes
not knowing there was still one final blow;
the jumper in the bottom drawer that Lou
had knitted all those years ago: each stitch
she'd said, a stitch of love. Now, frayed at the neck
and threadbare at the elbows, like his marriage,
he too, felt worn and torn, beyond repair.
He sobbed, as if to douse those fiery flames.
But tears don't work that way.
                           The flames that burnt
the sizzling wool when he tossed it into the fire,
like the flames that had burnt and scarred his face,
were now a part of his life.

Three generations had worked this land
that he'd been forced to sell.
A sense of loss and failure and shame
now fought in his inner hell.

Now they were selling his stock and plant,
a lifetime encapsulated
in tools used by his grandad dear,
and equipment he'd updated.

The silo he and his dad had built
now nearly full of grain,
the scales he'd bought with his first wool cheque,
and also his home-made crane.

Oh, how he longed to feel his dad
standing there next to him,
but then he was glad he wasn't around
to witness this sorrowful scene.

The sheep they'd worked so hard to breed
were going off God knows where,
as the raucous voice of the auctioneer
callously rent the air.

The mist grew heavy before his eyes,
his vision was not so clear,
for it's hard to see your world sold up,
and lose all that you hold dear.

When the phone call came he called to Bob;
We're on our way at last.
They're shearing down on Roo Lagoon,
there's six weeks' work at least.

I've always been told I'm good and fast,
I reckon this could be fun,
I'll be glad to get back to work again,
I might even be the gun.

So now, me mate, we're on our own,
we'll sing to the very same tune,
whether rich or poor, for better or worse,
it's now just me and you.

They're shearing down on Roo Lagoon,
all five stands are humming.
They're shearing down at Roo Lagoon,
the long blows swiftly coming.

Woolly backs in and off-shears out
while the fleece rides high in the air;
cries of 'Sheep-oh!' the shearers shout
while over the pen flies the rouseabout
to push up the wethers in there.

Shed hands deftly sweeping the floor
with a flick and a twist of the paddle,
throwing the fleeces, reaching for more,
'Keep the clip clean,' yells the boss in a roar
to those skirting the wool on the table.

Boss of the shed, the classer stands
surrounded by wool piled high.
On to the table another fleece lands
while the presser takes out the bales and brands
them ROO LAGOON K.I.,

triple AM or triple B,
bellies or pieces or stain,
they're cutting well this year, says he,
and right he is undoubtedly,
for they're never short of rain.

So summer is here and it's on once more,
the rush, the bustle, the smell,
the end of a year that they've laboured for
now briefly passes across the floor,
and they know that the job's done well.

Yes, they're shearing again on Roo Lagoon,
all five stands are humming,
and the end of the week at Roo Lagoon
will see their cut-out coming.

A shearer is an artist and a good one.
But he doesn't see it so. It's just a job
to him: he whistles up his dog to fetch the mob
and push them up the race for the next run,

then drags the first one out to trim the head,
the legs and belly, before, down on one knee
for the longest blow of all, his cutters free
the snow-white fleece upon the floor of the shed.

His body, muscles taught, with sweat on skin,
could be a Grecian hero from the past,
those winners of gold medals unsurpassed:
he too, could be a proud Olympian.

Just watching is to feel the deep emotion
of seeing something beautiful in motion.

After months of his embittered decline,
sometimes even losing his grip entirely,
Jim felt he'd come to the end of that grim road.

He stood up tall at No 1 stand
working linament into his muscles
as if it was a balm for wounded pride.
He'd show the world he was the best.

He knew nothing of the future,
of the new man on the team
and the challenge he was about to face.
But the final tally for that first day
foreshadowed what was soon to be
a battle royal in every way.

Tom Duggan was a nuggety man,
tough and wiry, his muscles attune
to the music of the humming sheds
and his cutters never missed a beat.
A shock of hair stood up, untamed,
like his vocabulary if challenged
on a point of disagreement. He rarely spoke
and when he did he looked intently into eyes
as if discerning what was meant, not what
was said. Some found this disconcerting.
He was much older than the others,
had come from interstate and travelled with
his daughter Emma, who was blind.
Their caravan was parked near Jim's
but neither felt that they were neighbours.
No conversation ever started. No words
came up to swim but drowned
before they even surfaced.
Communication was a sentence blotted out
except for Bob who wandered
where no words were needed.

Inevitably the Fates decreed
that only one could win.
And it did not take long.
Tom paced the younger Jim,
sheep for sheep,
until he'd proved to everyone
he was the better shearer,
not only fast but also clean;
he never nicked the body of a sheep.
When he moved up to No. 1
a brittle fury you could feel
hung from the rafters of the shed
like fragile glass about to shatter.
It was sensed by all. The tension grew.

Jim pushed the man who'd taken
what he'd just regained, determined
not to stay at No. 2 for long.
He pushed him hard.
He pushed him long.
He pushed him every blow.
He pushed him so
that Tom was fighting
every minute to outpace him.
Sweating bodies swayed in sync,
a mirror image none could crack until
Tom's handpiece took control.
Locked up, it skittered round the boards,
a wild thing, unpredictable, berserk.
Before the power could be turned off
its dance of death had left behind
Tom's leg severely damaged.
They could not stem the flow of blood,
so an ambulance was called.
Tom was no longer on the team
but in the hospital.

With Tom now gone and Emma on her own
the shearers rallied round, did what they could.
But it was Jim who did the most to help.
He checked her tank for water and fuel for the stove
and took her into town whenever needed.
He phoned each night to see how Tom was doing
and then they talked a while. He grew to like her.
Began to understand that what he thought
was beauty, skin deep only, without depth,
was nothing to the beauty he'd discovered
in the words of this young girl. His world
was slowly changing. Pity for himself
was now replaced by care for others, Emma
in particular. He needed all those nightly chats
to face what each day brought him
although as yet he did not know just why.

One evening, when he was weary from a hot
and hectic day, she came and stood behind him,
pressed her thumbs upon his shoulders,
massaged muscles slowly, with deliberation.
Why Jim, your muscles are all knotted.
Don't you know, to be a first-class shearer
you should let them flow? It's almost like
you've got a chip upon your shoulder.

At this his anger overflowed.
For Christ's sake, girl, if you could only see,
you'd understand!
                      But Jim, now you just listen.
I've heard the talk. I know what's happened to you,
about the fire, your wife and your divorce.
And I don't care about those facial scars,
it's all those scars inside I want to soothe.

And so he let her work upon him
every night, with gentleness,
accepting all she had to give with grace.

One night, sitting together in the cool of the evening
Jim asked Emma, Are you bitter, about being blind
I mean? Good heavens no, she said.
Why should I be? I feel that I can see
far better than most people. Some only see
the mask that hides the soul, but I perceive
behind that mask. It's what I call my second sight.
I've seen behind your mask and found your soul.
It's nicer than you realise, she said.
I just don't understand you, Jim replied.
To me it makes no bloody sense at all,
this second sight and people's masks. It's weird.
He stood, as if to go, but Emma spoke:

Then listen to this tale. In ancient Greece
there was a man, young Oedipus by name
who went to Delphi to find out his Fate,
his future if you like. That's how he learned
that he would kill his father, wed his mother
and beget four children. He was so horrified at this
he left his parents' home and wandered far away
so that these dreadful deeds could not occur.
But Fate was cruel. Unknown to this young man
the couple who had raised him weren't his parents.
Even worse, his travels led him to the two who were
so what had been foretold eventually came true.
Years later, when he learned the truth, he gouged
his eyes out of their sockets in despair
for they had led him to this dreadful act.

He spent his last years living like a hermit
with a priestly guide, Tiresias by name.
And it was only then he found his new insight:
the blind, you see, can see what can't be seen.

But Emma, you can't even read, so how
do you know all about this awful man?

My mother used to tell me tales before
she died and then there's always books you know,
in Braille. That's where my fingers are my eyes.
I get my books on loan from Adelaide.
I'll show you one I'm reading now, *The Hobbit*.
See how the pages are not smooth but raised
in different marks, and I know what they mean,
although a sighted person couldn't read a word.
Can you see now that eyes alone are not
what people need to see what's really there?

Intrigued about her reading
he ran his fingers over several pages.
Two hundred years ago, she said,
a man called Louis Braille
invented this new language;
just six small dots is all it takes,
six small raised dots,
two rows of three, like the side of a dice
or a domino block. That's where it starts.
Different combinations of these dots
create the alphabet, some common words
and syllables, a whole new world.
Yes, it does take time to learn
but that is not the hardest task.
The hardest part is learning sense of touch
to recognise those many variations.
Your fingers need to be as sensitive
as fluttering butterflies seeking nectar.
You'd be quite good you know,
you shearers have the softest skin
working all day in that lanolin.

Later, she asked about his parents.
Is that something you can't share?
He was glad she couldn't see his face,
his pain so hard to bare.

Mum died when I was still at school,
from cancer, I've been told.
And Dad – well, a truckie took him out
coming round the bend

on the wrong side of the road, not far
from here. He never had a chance.
A year before the fire he died.
I still can't bear to glance

at that sad spot. I go the long
way round and think I always will,
just to avoid my memories of loss.
You've got your father still –

but I have no one. Not a soul.
Oh yes, you have. There's always me.
She put her hands up to his face
and stroked it, lovingly.

For she knew too, how sad it was
to lose someone you loved so much,
a caring friend, whose memory
one could no longer touch.

It helped her to tell Jim about
the mother who had been her guide
around a sightless world and then
had suddenly just died.

The breeze blew softly on lips that spoke
of silent grief, that undertone
of haunting loss. And both soon knew
they were no longer alone.

That night he could not sleep.
Unanswered questions like falling leaves,
smothered his restless body,
kept him awake with their noiseless noise.
This girl was not like any he had known.
So gentle and so genuine.
She did not drink or sleep around,
and every word she said was meant for him,
or so it seemed, as if she were a teacher.
The words she spoke, the things she said,
hung round him, out of reach,
like misremembered echoes of a dream,
a dream he hoped one day to catch.

Their sunset chats were now
the best part of his day.
Each evening, when coloured curtains
ruched the western sky,
Emma cooked for two.
Later they would wander
where the curlews called at night.
Jim marvelled how she managed
in this world without her sight
and noticed on their walks how Bob
would gently nudge her from
an obstacle that might cause her to trip
as if he were a guide dog.
His dog just knew what he must do
for her. He envied that,
decided he would try to be the same.

You've got a good dog there
she said to Jim one night,
stroking the head that rested on her feet.
I listen when you work the sheep,
you hardly ever need to speak,
especially with ewes and lambs.
He's gentle, doesn't rush them,
seems to know, instinctively,
just what he has to do,
like he's got second sight.
Don't start on that again, he laughed.
Instinctively, she knew to say no more.

I'll never be able to understand
the half of what she knows.
Oh, how I would like to discover
just what makes her so.

There's something about her I can't let go,
there's something I feel is rare,
and I really don't care how long it takes
just so long as she's always there

for me each night when I get home.
I'm sure she feels the same,
although she's never said. But then
some feelings can't be named.

The curlews were calling, the night was still.
Moonbeams flew through the star-struck air,
as she lay there longing to say, 'I will.'

She dreamt that the curlews' cry would fulfil
her youthful dreams, her unsung prayer,
for the curlews call when the night is still

and she knew that was when a young girl's will,
her dearest wish, would be granted there
where her heart would one day say, 'I will'.

She reached for the moon and stars until
her thoughts became an unspoken prayer.
The curlews were calling, the night was still.

The calls went on. The calls were shrill.
They entered her heart. They rent the air.
She knew they wanted to say, 'I will.'

In a dream she entered a mist-clad chill
while moonbeams flew through the star-struck air.
The curlews were calling, the night was still
and she cried at last, 'I will, I will.'

It had been a scorching day
and the heat still hung around at night
sucking all the moisture it could find
from man and beast and land.
Let's go to Snellings Beach for a swim,
Jim said. I'd love to, she replied,
but I have never swum, you know.
Come on. I'll teach you then.
You'll feel like a different person.

When they arrived the setting sun,
a blaze of Indian silk,
wrapped round her like a scarf.
Its left-over warmth on the sand
pushed up between her toes,
something sharp and clean on her skin
she had never felt before.
It seemed to her the sea was laughing
as it swirled around her feet
in a game of hide and seek
that sucked and glugged. Come on.
They stripped down to their undies.
Then he took her hand to guide her
into the depths of that vast ocean,
into the salty-smelling sea,
into a world where she'd never been.

She lay her damp clothes
on a nearby bush to dry,
revelled in the new-found feel
of salt slowly drying on her skin
like a delicate tissue.
Happiness covered her body
in an unseen smile.
Let's swim here every night, she said,
reaching out to find his hand and hold it.
Tenderly, gently, he began to caress her
as if unwrapping a fragile gift,
whose beauty he dare not mar.

And before the sickle moon had set
at the base of the starless heavens,
she had given him, with all her love,
the most precious gift of all.

They slept until the Sunday sun
awoke them with the warmth of Matins.
Awoke them as two different people.
This is a lovers' beach, she said,
scooping up a handful of sand,
letting it trickle through her fingers.
This sand, you know, is the grit and grain
that comes from years of storms
pounding on delicate shells
until it has become as deep
as the depth of the love
I feel for you.
As I do too, he said,
his trembling voice
replacing the words
he could not find to say.

He was a simple man, not one well-versed.
Barely articulate. Tripped over words
like stumbling blocks. Misread their meaning,
leaning as they did at awkward angles
in their sentences. Preferred to disentangle
fencing wire or fishing line,
not convoluted letters of the mind.

And yet, between his workman's hands there grew
a wordless song that flew each time he looked upon
his life, his love. His touch wrote poetry he knew
she understood. No need for metre, assonance or rhyme.
No cause to write, recite, communicate by mail.
At night his fingers traced unwritten lines,
translating as he went, his text to Braille.

Like a lost man stumbling
through a darkened forest
he'd come upon a patch of light
he had not known existed.

This love he felt for Emma was unlike
the shallowness he'd known before.
It was so deep he could not fathom
how it came about
but knew for certain
it would not leave him, ever.

Their nightly trysts did not pass by
unnoticed by the others in the team
who talked about what might occur
when Tom discovered what had
happened while he was away.
Not much was said to Jim
for they could see he'd changed,
that Emma, as a person, was his main concern,
not just their nightly trysts.
It's almost like he's someone else
they said. He never used to be
so gentle and so caring with the girls.

When Tom came back they took him to the pub,
tried to tell him gently what had happened,
how happy Emma was, that Jim had taken care
of everything she needed. But in spite of all,
Tom read between the lines and guessed just what
was going on. He stormed out of the pub,
hurried home to find his van was empty.
Jim's FJ wasn't there.
Tom left for Snellings Beach.

The beach was wide and empty
but Jim's car was parked nearby.
Tom walked along the sand dunes
by the beach, and when he saw
what they were doing his anger
burst like a pent-up dam.
He grabbed Jim by the hair
and punched him several times.
You fuckin' bastard, he cried out,
get off my fuckin' daughter.
With that he kicked
the young man in the groin,
sent through his body paralysing shocks
that made Jim think he never would
make love again. He doubled up
in agony. Heard Tom call out,
For God's sake get your clothes on, girl,
and then he heard them leave.

They drove to Roo Lagoon in silence,
shrouded in the heavy weight of anger.
Once back in the van, his daughter challenged him.
I'll thank you, Dad, to never use that word again
for something that I know is beautiful.
Good God, girl, you ain't married
he cried out. And nor were you, she parried,
when you first loved my mother.
I know the dates. That shut him up.
And anyway, I am you know,
married in the eyes of God, I mean.
Not mine, you ain't.
He looked at her and saw
the fiery woman he'd once loved
now living in his daughter.
He'd heard those words before.
Besides, we plan to marry when we can.
No priest would marry someone who's divorced.
Then there's a civil wedding, she replied.
But that would not be in a church!
At that her anger burst its chains.
Could I but see you now, I'd throw
this saucepan just to silence you.
You haven't been to mass
since mother passed away.
The church means nothing to you now.
You don't believe a single word they say.
So just shut up.

But he had one last point to make.
Now Emma, love, can you not see
it's just because
he knows you cannot see him
that he's had his way with you.
You're blind, girl, you're disabled…
As the saucepan hit the wall,
fell down and broke a pile of plates,
she yelled, Disabled!
Don't ever use that word again.
I am not disabled.
I can see far better than most people.
Dad, don't say another word,
just let me be.

The tension in the shed next day
was a physical presence that bound them all.
Jim's bruises told them who had won the fight
and even when they'd disappeared
days later, Tom's fury carried on.
He watched the young man's every move,
kept him from his daughter
and never spoke a word.

When cut-out came in ten days' time
and they all sat around with a beer,
Jim said what he'd wanted to say for days:
I want to marry your daughter, Tom,
I can't go on without her.
Over my dead body, the answer came,
I'll see you first in Hell.
You're nothing but a fuckin' bastard
and a bloody monster as well.

But Emma had a trump card up her sleeve.
Before we leave, she said, for our next shed,
I want to speak to Jim, with you.
Will you get him or I?

She faced her father.
Stood in front of Jim,
the man she loved,
pulled his arms around her,
held on tight.
I want you to arrange
a trip to Adelaide for us three,
so Jim and I can marry.
And before you blow your top,
you need to know I'm pregnant.
Jim's arms around her tightened,
felt her belly, warm and soft, alive
with the promise of new life.
You bastard, Tom cried out.
You bloody bastard.
Then just make sure
your grandchild isn't one as well.
He couldn't answer that.
She smiled. Thanks, Dad, she said.

Thank God the balloon's been busted,
the classer said. Such tension
in the team just isn't good,
as we've already seen.
I'm sure that's why
Tom's hand-piece took control.

So now, let's have a party
for the happy couple.
I'll pass the hat around
so we can buy them something
special for their wedding.
I know I'm not the only one
has got a soft spot for those two.

So they went out hunting for wild pigs,
set up two spits to cook them on,
and then lit fires in four big pits,
to roast the spuds in iron camp ovens.
The kitchens in the neighbourhood
were just as busy turning out
their very special party food
for which they were all famed:
pavlovas and quandong pies,
lamingtons and jelly tarts,
not to mention piles of cream puffs,
chocolate cakes and sponges too.
Meanwhile, in the nearby shed
the scene was one of transformation
when the local netball team
arrived with all their decorations.
Streamers snaked down from the rafters,
in all the colours of the rainbow
while balloons like bursting udders
shuddered in a gentle glow.
Buckets full of flowers waltzed in,
perfume floating in the air,
trying hard to mask the smell of
sheep-shit 'neath the slatted floor.
When the sun pulled up its bedsheets
logs of wood replaced its warmth
as thrills of heightened expectation
like a bright electric cord
wove through all the decorations
calling guests to Come, Enjoy.

Kegs were opened, food was served,
and when they could no longer eat,
they called out for the local band
to satisfy their itchy feet.
A lager phone, accordion
wash-board and a violin,
started up their dancing music
loud enough to raise the roof.
Soon the floor boards were vibrating
to the beat of RM boots,
polished up and newly shining
like they'd never shone before.
Oh what fun, this wining, dining.
Oh what joy this raucous singing.
Oh the many glasses toasting,
Jim and Emma, here's to you.
They danced until the wee small hours,
they danced and sang in tune and out.
It was a party to remember,
like welcome clouds that break the drought.

Back in the days when stonemasons and brickies
took infinite pride in their work, this building,
now used to register all births and deaths
as well as civil weddings, took on a
benevolent aura that smiled upon
all those who came to plight their troth.

Jim arrived with a bunch of roses, Lorraine Lee,
chosen solely for their perfume and with thorns
removed so Emma would not hurt herself.
She buried her face in the flowers
to inhale their aroma,
her smile opening up to the world
like a bud opening up to the sun.
Perhaps I have misjudged him after all,
Tom wondered to himself
as Jim gave him a buttonhole.
Thanks, son, he said. Good luck.
Then he grabbed Jim's hand, and shook it,
as if he were sealing a deal.
Let's get started, eh?

They drove to Victor Harbor
for their honeymoon,
each day a day of discovery.
Sometimes, after making love,
she let her fingers wander over
the patina of his scars
as if reading a road map.
I'm glad of that fire, she smiled.
It's brought something to the surface
you didn't know you had because
your life was just too easy.
You never had to face a single test
or overcome adversity till then.

You might be right, he said

                      But deep down
he was glad she could not see his face.

At last, the battleground was cleared,
a kind of truce declared.
At their next shed both vans
stood side by side, connected by
a line of conversation,
the only difference being
Emma moved from Tom's van
into Jim's.
Tom, hampered by his damaged leg
ceded top position in the shed
to the man he'd once derided
as that 'bloody ugly monster'
and who was now
his son-in-law.

Tom's first impressions
slowly changed.
He could not help but see
the love that shone from
Jim's adoring eyes
and wrapped his daughter
in a universe she'd never known –
and how it changed her.
An enlightenment
for all to see.

Determined not to lose the scent
that flavoured her wedding vows,
Emma bought a very large pot
to plant her 'memory flowers'.

She sought advice from friends she knew,
just how the soil should be,
and when she had done all she was told
she planted her rose, a Lorraine Lee.

When Jim came home and saw her wounds
where thorns had torn her skin
he gently washed the blood away
from where those cuts had been.

Don't worry about my hands she said,
those nicks I can hardly feel,
and it's worth it to have my special rose;
those thorns are no big deal.

For she could remember a villanelle,
her mother's favourite poem;
framed on the wall above her bed,
it had been the heart of their home.

'Life is like honey, dripping on thorns,
soothing and smoothing, a poem soft told,
healing the wounds to which we were born.

With heartache and injury, bleeding and torn,
reach for the humming hive's rich, golden glow.
Life is like honey, dripping on thorns.

Without the scars of His rough crown of thorns
Christ could not give us His promise foretold:
the healing of wounds to which we are born.

Darkness and death we need no longer mourn,
for death is not final, its sting can't withhold
a life that is honey, dripping on thorns.

Life gives us joy, and to joy we're reborn
when the warmth and aroma of flowers unfold,
healing the wounds to which we are born.

So savour the honey, the balm of the swarm
look into its mirror yourself to behold
healing the wounds to which we were born
life is pure honey dripping on thorns.'

And so the season turns autumnal,
a slowly rolling wheel whose spokes,
in the setting sun, stretch out
like strips of egg and bacon on a plate,
awaiting the dishwasher of night.
Sitting outside in the evening glow
he reaches over, rests his hand
on her slowly swelling belly,
longing for the day when movement
will verify the wonder of new life.
Her face glows, like a bud,
blossoms at the touch of his hand.
A feeling he is unable to explain
slowly nets and knots him
in a tapestry of gentleness and love.
He would like to tell her this
but he cannot find the words.
So he settles for:
I'll do the dishes tonight.

There were times he couldn't
take his eyes from his wife.
Through her, he'd changed,
now noticed things that some might miss
although he kept them to himself.
He knew the glow that all could see
came from a unique fulfilment.
Not only the instrument of his desire,
she was as well the means
by which their love would
manifest itself to all.
And he remembered his dear Gran
sitting him upon her knee
when he was just a child,
and telling him that life
holds many different kinds of love,
not just desire but loyal friendship, honour,
worship and respect as well as that
which shines from parents' eyes
and never wavers. A selfless love
that is its own reward.

I am no longer the flower of the dark
where life is not.
I am the fruit of the root
where life begins,
the unknown quantity
between conception and birth.
I cannot see or hear or speak
but my genes reverberate
like the ringing sound
of hammer on anvil
forging a form unique to me
with the flaming heat of a passionate fire
I did not light but must submit to.
And when my birth unties that corded knot
of blinding sight and deafening sound,
I will at last both hear and see
those two whose light now shines in me.

One night Jim dreamt that he was playing football.
He'd never played a better game.
He felt like the star of the universe –
he'd kicked five goals and everyone was cheering.
With the optimism that only a dream can give,
he thought his team might even win – for once.
They needed one more goal in just one minute.
He lined it up, was about to aim and kick
when something knocked him right off balance
and what had been a certain goal
was just a sad and sorrowful behind.
When he awoke he knew just what
had pushed him out of kilter:
the jerking movements 'neath his hand
like words that might have been shorthand,
were but a foetal Morse code known
for having a definite mind of its own.

There was something about the way he slammed the car door.
An exclamation mark at the end of a sentence?
Even before he sat down beside her, words came tumbling out
like tools from a toolbox, waiting to be sorted:
the bloke who bought my farm – a city guy – his wife wants to leave –
but he wants to keep it as an investment – probably a tax deduction –
wants me to manage it for him – he'll pay well – and I can do what
I like with the back paddock. Oh Emma, don't you see? I can go home.
I can take my family home. Our children can grow up where I was born.
Do you understand just how much this means to me?
And one day I'll buy my old farm back. You'll see.
There was no question mark at the end of that sentence.

So they went to Adelaide in the ute
to buy what they would need
and Emma paid a visit to
the Institute for the Blind
and her doctor, to discuss her future.
Reassured, she came back home
as calm as a windless day,
as cool as an autumn evening.
But Jim was not so settled.
He could not wait to return
to the home where he was born.
He danced and darted here and there,
like a frisky foal on a frosty morning,
Only three more days before we move,
he said. Then two. I just can't wait.
And then the final day arrived.
His words tripped over themselves
in his excitement, as if they couldn't see
where they were going, like his wife,
who was feeling her way, slowly,
into this new and foreign world.
Don't worry, she said.
I'm getting there.

She'd never heard her man so happy.
Realised that losing his farm
had left a different kind of scar,
one that spread out like an aching bruise
but which was now receding.
His past, tied up, was now connected
to his future in the present of his being.
I can't tell you what it means to me
to give you a decent home, he said,
a home that's always been a happy one
and will be still. I know.
Can you not feel it? She smiled.
I've felt a lot of things today.

Not only did she feel the furniture,
remember its position and its function,
but learnt as well which pieces
had a story of their own to tell.
They spoke to her as she read them
like a page of Braille,
polishing hard until they smiled
with the shine of their timber
and smell of the wax.

My grandad made that chest of drawers,
Jim told her, this table and that chair,
from a big old walnut tree that died.
It's not dead, Jim, Emma replied.
It's living, now, with us.
And she rubbed even harder,
as if to release a genie.

Like a prince showing off his realm
Jim drove his wife all over the farm,
walked her through the shelter belts,
along the creeks that were usually dry
and described, with the keenness of a farmer's eye,
the quality of sheep she could but hear and feel.
If only you could see it, Emma.
After the winter rain, it looks like Paradise.

Well, I can feel the change in you, she said,
as if it was ablaze like those neon lights
you talk about when we visit the city.
That makes me very happy. I don't need sight
to see our home. I can feel it putting its arms
around me. Now, show me the shearing shed.

This is the heart of the farm, he said,
carrying her up the steps like a bride
and putting her gently down on the boards
where every year the wool clip was scored.
My dad redesigned it before he died
to make a much more efficient shed,
we put in chutes by each shearer's stand
and widened the boards for more shed hands.

Then the yards outside also needed repair
so we rebuilt them all as bugle yards,
they're curved, you know, and so the sheep,
without those threatening corners, keep
much calmer running through the yards.
You'd be amazed how easy they scare,
there are times, you know, when they drive you insane,
although I suppose I shouldn't complain

because they are still my chosen career.
I love the feel of a well-bred sheep –
a micron's that fine – a flesh that is firm –
a wool-cheque that keeps me safe from the storm –
and I swear to you, love, there's one promise I'll keep,
I'll buy back this farm that to me is so dear.
I'll make that my goal, what you'd call my quest –
and as for tonight, I'll cook tea while you rest.

The days now hung around her
like a dainty shawl of lace,
its weightless warmth a cosy comfort.
No longer moving from shed to shed
she was now considered a local.
Women came to welcome her
to their community,
brought gifts for the coming birth
and wrapped her in an undemanding
friendship, that grew, like her belly, daily.
Each time the infant moved
she felt him settling in, like her,
into a down-lined nest.

I've been floating in this fluid
all my life it seems, but now
something tells me
it's time to surface.
I do not know
if I am on time
when time is like life,
and never stands still
but rolls on forever,
a river of dreams,
dreams that some weep for,
dreams that some wait for
and dreams that
flow out to the sea.
But wherever I am
on this river of dreams,
this moment, this hour,
will no longer wait.
The choice is not mine,
that is one thing I know,
for something now tells me
I really must go.

Even in his absence
the room was full of his presence.
Even before the first signs of arrival
she knew it would not be long.
The night was filled with
the glorious wonder of ghosts
who'd trod that way before.
They led her, step by step,
along the path of pleasure and pain,
the road that led to wonder and joy
of greeting a life so beautifully made.

A boy, they said, placing him in her arms,
and she thought, if that's what it is
to have a baby, I could do it
every day of the week.

When Jim bent down in awe
to stroke that peach-like cheek,
a tiny fist grabbed his finger, as if
hanging on for dear life.
How can anything be so perfect,
he thought. Then said,
Let's call him Tommy.

Life went on like a formal dance,
stepping automatically to the music of life,
rarely out of tune.

They'd learned their steps full well
and when another came to join them,
following the well-known pattern,
their feet slipped lightly into
different steps like winter days
that slip into their summer length with ease.
Hands that once held one another
now took a younger pair to add
a different rondo to their dance,
one to teach as it was taught,
one to reap as it was wrought.

Jim's wonder at the sight of his son
grew like clover in spring,
enveloping him in future hope
for what this joy would bring.

But his wonder was always tempered by
the one thing he could not do,
for his dream would only be complete
if Emma could see him too.

And then the letter came.

Jim read it out to Emma:
Referring to my visit – I'm pleased to say –
it's very new – but we are optimistic –
already two successful operations –
in two weeks' time – we've booked you in.

What does this mean? Jim asked of Emma,
looking at the letter, puzzled and bewildered.
When I was last in Adelaide, she replied,
they told me they were just about
to try an operation that could possibly
restore the sight to people like myself.
As it was still unproven, I didn't say a word.
I didn't want to raise your hopes. Besides,
I know the fear you hold inside
and won't admit, not even to yourself,
but now I think it's time to put all that aside.
We have another to consider.
Just think of our son, Tommy.
It may not be successful but
we should at least give it a try
for his sake, don't you think?
So I can watch and care for him
like other mothers?

Like the granting of wishes in fairy tales
where there's often a darker side,
Jim couldn't help but fear and dread
what hope might one day bring.

He thought of his son, how much safer he'd be
if his mother could watch, not just listen.
And Emma herself. Why shouldn't she see
the beauty that fate had denied her?

Of course he agreed with everyone else
what a wonderful gift this would be,
yet a question mark hung like a noose in his mind
in spite of his hopes and his pleas.

For if Emma was able to see their son,
as he had so often wished,
then she would be able to see him too,
in all his ugliness.

Jim had no love of hospitals,
no pleasant soothing memories
of healing feelings, care and comfort.
He'd watched his mother fade and shrivel
into sheets as white as her until
she disappeared completely from his world.
Then his father, bloodied, lifeless,
couldn't even say goodbye
when there was still so much to say.
And his few months some years ago:
doctors slicing off his skin
like peeling par-boiled sausages.
Oh the pain of those wounds
and the wounds of that pain
and the face of his wife,
God, not that again.

So Emma understood Jim's reasons
for not staying in the city
for her operation. That his words,
'I need to check the ewes each day,
we're lambing soon you know'
were just his way of saying,
'God knows what you will think
when you see me as I am.'

They knew this operation
could be life-changing
for them both. What if,
Jim thought, when Emma's eyes
are opened to the world
as I have always known it,
she sees it from a different point of view,
a perspective that might change
the way we live and love?

His thoughts were so tied up in knots
he could not string them out coherently.

When the phone call came
to say that all had been successful
it seemed to Jim that those few words
were stuck inside the wires.
He could not grasp them
with both hands, and later,
when he could, there were
but two that he could find:
just 'hope' and 'fear'.

The ward is a happy place today.
The word 'success' hangs in the air
like the breath of a new idea.
But I am not as happy as the nurses.
The world that I once knew by feel
now glares with alien eye at me, as if
I've come from some far distant country
and must learn to speak another language
before it will accept me as its own.
What I once recognised in spite of
what it lacked is now disguised or
hidden by that very lack, its colour,
that overwhelming, blinding presence
that is so foreign to me. It is
an unfamiliar world I now inhabit.
I feel I am a foreigner.
Even the lovely roses in this vase
that Jim has sent me, once known
for their aroma and their
petal-touch of silken softness,
now blind me with their colour.
I need to close my eyes to see them
as they really are.
And yet, I love that colour.
They tell me it's called pink.

So I am what they call a blue-eyed blonde?
But that can be confusing. They tell me
that the colour of the sky is also blue, but
I have watched it change throughout the day,
like water rippling over my feet,
so many variations. Are they all blue?

And then there's green. A nurse took me
to the Botanic Gardens yesterday
where everything is green,
the trees, the plants, the grass.
All greens but not the same.

Don't get me wrong. I'm not complaining.
It's just that colours come in such variety
I need to learn a new vocabulary.
But don't they make the world
a beautiful place? A living symphony
of variations, all in harmony.
I never could have visualised it so.

I know that's a ring, a circle,
because I've felt that shape before.
And I know it is a carrot
because I've often eaten them.
But what do you call that brilliant colour?
Orange, they said. How bright this orange.
Orange. She pronounced it
as if learning a different language.
And they added, like apricots in summer,
you know, or pumpkin. But the brightest
of all is the fruit called orange.
I'll get you one if you like.

A perfect sphere in her hand
the orange glistened in her vision
reflecting its own wonder in her eyes.
Would you like me to peel it for you?
No thank you. Not yet.
That night she went to sleep,
holding it in her hands,
dreaming of the orange tree
Jim had just planted.

My lanterns float in a pool of leaves,
cut through the air with autumn's eye
and light the way to winter's solstice.
I mould the wax of the ivory moon
until it is full, delicious and ripe.
When you peel me, feel my flesh firm
to your touch. Let my juices fill
your mouth with summer madness.
In the harem of your garden I am called
Favourite. I bring the sun to your bed.

Come on there, mate, it's time to go
to see what seems to me a miracle
I never thought I'd see.
But Jim did not reply, just stood
as if snap-frozen on the spot.

Then Tom saw something
he had never seen before.
Jim's scars became a scree of stones,
an avalanche of anguish fed by
two sad rivulets of tears.

I can't, he said, I just can't go.
I know she's not like Lou
but still, I'm terrified I'll see
her lovely face freeze over
with horror and revulsion
like happened once before.
I can't erase that memory.

And there's one other thing;
I know for certain,
when she sees me
that first time,
I want to be alone with her,
with her and no one else.

Tom, whose world had always been
the sort where grown men never cry,
was at a loss for words.
He didn't share Jim's fears
but knew that this was not the time
to challenge him.
With Tommy in his arms, he said,
All right, we'll go without you.
But she'll be home in two weeks' time.
You'll have to face her then.

I've never seen a bloke so cut up, Emma.
He sobbed and sobbed, just wouldn't come.
I'm sorry, love.

Don't worry, Dad. I understand.
He's had a hard few years.
Like that book of myths and legends
Mother used to read to me,
he's had tough tests to pass.
But pass them all he has, with help
from me of course, she smiled.
You know the scars that matter,
those inside? I've healed them all.
He's now a different man.
Just wait till I get back, you'll see,
we'll pass the final test together,
come out with flying colours
like the sunset I saw yesterday.
You know, Dad, all those colours
I didn't know existed?
Oh, how blindingly beautiful they were.

Jim, you should have seen her
when she first saw Tommy.
Laughed and cuddled him,
felt every inch of his face
with her fingers, just to recognise him first,
and then, her smile, oh that smile.
She looked like one of them madonnas
you see in churches, you know,
all that coloured glass in windows,
or a statue in a chapel.
She couldn't get enough of him,
just ate him with her eyes, she did.
I tell you now, son, my daughter's
the nearest thing to an angel you can get.
She won't do anything to hurt you.
God's honour, I know that for certain.

'You'll have to face her then.'
Tom's words hung in his ears for days,
ringing and singing, out of reach,
and loud. Too loud. He could not
turn them down, however hard he tried.
He wondered about that word 'face',
how it was used at times:
'about face', 'face the music' and
'you'll just have to face it' –
the implied inevitability of the word –
like his own face, now cracked and dried,
resembling the bottom of a drought-fed dam,
that can never be erased, no matter
how much rain might fall.

It seemed just like a day or two
had passed when Tom came up:
I'm going to fetch her now, he said.
I'll take young Tommy with me
and keep him for an hour or two
so you can both be alone for a while.

He was down by the dam where she knew he would be,
squatting on his heels, head in his hands,
as if about to curl into a ball and hide,
like an echidna rolling inside protective spines.
Dressed in his work jeans and Blundstone boots,
he'd done nothing to spruce himself up,
hadn't even combed his hair, for he felt
that wasn't part of the deal, the test he had to face.
Frozen, like a statue, he could hardly move.
Fear and hope were tearing him apart,
turning him inside out. He shivered,
as if his clothes were too flimsy
to give him any comfort at all,
as if he needed his Drizabone to keep warm,
shelter him from the oncoming storm.

She arrived, soft-footed and silent as a feather,
but Bob's welcome told him she was there.
Turn round and face me, Jim, she said.
And when he did, she gently stroked,
with warm and loving hands,
that rough and bumpy road he'd travelled
those past two years, until she'd covered it
with a surface of her own devising.
I love you, Jim McFarlane, she said.
You look just like the man I fell in love with.

They went to the pub for tea that night,
all four of them. The noise when they arrived
reminded Emma of a neighbour's television,
the night Mick Jagger walked on stage.

Like radiant sunflowers faces turned towards her.
She knew them all by voice, her sight now adding
physical traits she knew came from within,
those tell-tale lines of love and laughter.

The men playing darts called out to her:
Here, Emma, they said. Come and have a go.
And when she scored a bullseye second
time around, they voted her on their team.

Jim, cuddling young Tommy as if he were
a treasure beyond compare, felt he would
burst with pride, not only because he loved
her so but because she still loved him.

That night, as they lay in the nakedness of love,
in the sadness and gladness and madness of love,
words he'd never spoken before
fell from Jim's lips like evening dew
that arrives unannounced.

You are the flower of my life, he said,
a rose whose perfume never fades,
even when the petals fall
and whose thorns, dripping with honey,
sweeten my life every day.

Oh, Jim, she said,
where did you find those lovely words?
Through you, he said, through you.

He
could not feel her eyes
upon his back,
so he turned.

She,
with wings of grace
brushing against desire,
reached towards
his backward glance
but slipped and fell
into a bowl of stars
where words do not exist.

Curve of her cheek
still lies between
the sickle moon
and a young man's dream.

www.ingramcontent.com/pod-product-compliance
Lightning Source LLC
Chambersburg PA
CBHW070929080526
44589CB00013B/1450